# THE STORY BEHIND

# PLASTIC

Christin Ditchfield

Raintree

**www.raintreepublishers.co.uk**
Visit our website to find out more information about Raintree books.

**To order:**
☎ Phone 0845 6044371
🖨 Fax +44 (0) 1865 312263
✉ Email myorders@raintreepublishers.co.uk

Customers from outside the UK please telephone +44 1865 312262

Raintree is an imprint of Capstone Global Library Limited, a company incorporated in England and Wales having its registered office at 7 Pilgrim Street, London, EC4V 6LB – Registered company number: 6695582

Edited by Megan Cotugno and Diyan Leake
Designed by Philippa Jenkins
Original illustrations © Capstone Global
  Library Ltd (2011)
Illustrated by Philippa Jenkins
Picture research by Hannah Taylor and Mica Brancic
Originated by Capstone Global Library Ltd
Printed and bound in China by CTPS

ISBN 978 1 406 22926 4 (hardback)
15 14 13 12 11
10 9 8 7 6 5 4 3 2 1

ISBN 978 1 406 22940 0 (paperback)
16 15 14 13 12
10 9 8 7 6 5 4 3 2 1

**British Library Cataloguing in Publication Data**
Ditchfield, Christin.
  The story behind plastic. -- (True stories)
  668.4-dc22
A full catalogue record for this book is available from the British Library.

**Acknowledgements**
We would like to thank the following for permission to reproduce photographs: Alamy p. **20** (© Marcelo Rudini); Corbis pp. **16** (Peter Ginter), **23** (REUTERS/ Luke MacGregor); Getty Images pp. **5** (Science & Society Picture Library), **6** (Three Lions), **24** (Bloomberg/ Chip Chipman); istockphoto pp. **18** (© Skip O Donnell), **21** (© Miguel Malo); NASA p. **12**; Science Photo Library p. **27** (Paul Rapson); Shutterstock pp. **iii** (© Jiri Hera), **4** (© Seregam), **7** (© ARENA Creative), **8** (© nadi555), **9** (© Irina Silayeva), **10** (© vladm), **14** (© Elena Schweitzer), **15** (© indianstockimages), **19** (© Maridav), **11** (© Maxim Ahner), **13** (© Mircea Bezergheanu), **22** (© Perov Stanislav), **25** (© Konstantin Yolshin), **26** (© Stéphane Bidouze).

Cover photograph of drinking straws reproduced with permission of istockphoto/© Rob Eyers.

We would like to thank Ann Fullick for her invaluable help in the preparation of this book.

Every effort has been made to contact copyright holders of material reproduced in this book. Any omissions will be rectified in subsequent printings if notice is given to the publisher.

# Contents

Some words are shown in bold, **like this**.
You can find out what they mean by
looking in the glossary on page 30.

# An amazing invention

▲ All these things are made of plastic.

**What's in a name?**

The word *plastic* comes from the Greek word *plastikos*. It means "something that can be shaped or moulded".

Plastic – it's everywhere! Put this book down and look around you. You'll probably see at least 15 things made of plastic: a pen, your rucksack, jacket, shoes, a drink cup or water bottle, a snack wrapper, a CD or DVD, a ball, a bookshelf, markers, and a whiteboard.

Plastic is a material made of plants, wood fibres, or oil. With heat and pressure, it can be moulded into all kinds of shapes and used to make all kinds of objects – from toys to traffic lights to bullet-proof vests. Plastic has changed the way we live.

# The Great International Exhibition

At the 1862 Great International Exhibition in London, an Englishman called Alexander Parkes introduced a new product he called Parkesine. It was the first plastic that anyone had made. Parkes explained that this hard, solid substance became soft and flexible when it was heated. It could be shaped into tools and other useful objects. It could also be used to coat other objects and make them water-**resistant**.

▼ British chemist and inventor Alexander Parkes created the first human-made plastic.

## Alexander Parkes (1813–1890) ✔

Alexander Parkes was born in Birmingham in 1813. He won a bronze medal at the 1862 Great International Exhibition for his invention of Parkesine. He had originally been trying to find a replacement for ivory (the material that elephant tusks are made of). Parkes loved inventing new things and had **patents** (rights) on many of his inventions. He also fathered 20 children!

# The history of plastic

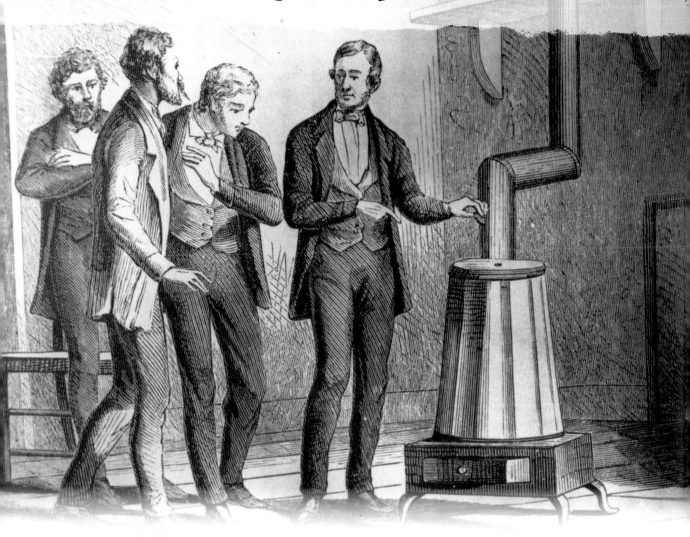

▲ The Goodyear Tire and Rubber Company was named in honour of Charles Goodyear and the work that he did to improve the qualities of natural rubber.

Rubber is a natural plastic. It comes from the milky sap of rubber trees. In 1839, the US inventor Charles Goodyear conducted experiments with rubber. He wanted to see if he could improve its qualities or **characteristics**. Natural rubber is sticky. It gets soft and gooey in the heat. It gets hard and snaps or breaks in the cold.

Goodyear discovered that heating rubber with a **chemical** (substance) called sulphur changed the texture. It made the rubber strong, elastic (stretchy), and waterproof. Now this rubber could be used for things like tyres, shoe soles, garden hoses, and even ice hockey pucks!

## More natural plastics

With Goodyear's **vulcanization** process, scientists created a hard, black rubber called vulcanite or ebonite. It was used to make combs and brushes, buttons, jewellery, and eventually bowling balls. In 1839, a German scientist called Eduard Simon discovered an oily, jelly-like plastic that came from the Turkish sweet gum tree. He called it **polystyrene**. Today a chemical form of polystyrene is used to make food and drink containers, packaging materials, **disposable** razors, and CD jewel cases.

In 1856, the US inventors Alfred Critchlow and Samuel Peck found that the female lac bug (a tiny insect found in the forests of India and Thailand) oozes a sticky liquid called resin. When the resin is dissolved in alcohol, it creates a clear liquid coating that hardens and protects the surfaces of wood and other substances. They called this coating shellac.

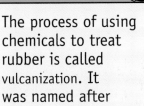

**Trial by fire**

The process of using chemicals to treat rubber is called vulcanization. It was named after Vulcan, the Roman god of fire.

◀ Different kinds of plastic are used to make disposable eating utensils and food and drink containers.

 Film is made from a kind of plastic called celluloid.

## A winning discovery

In 1863, a US inventor called John Wesley Hyatt read about a contest offering $10,000 (about £6,000 in today's money) to anyone who could come up with a new material for making billiard balls. At the time, billiard balls were made of ivory, which comes from elephant tusks. Ivory was getting too expensive and too difficult to find.

Hyatt won the contest with his invention of celluloid, a mixture of wood fibres and a waxy substance called camphor. Celluloid turned out to be a much more important discovery than Hyatt first realized. This new plastic was soon used for taking photographs and making films.

# The age of plastics

Dr Leo Hendrick Baekeland (1863–1944) was a US chemistry professor who wanted to improve on the inventions of ebonite, shellac, and celluloid. In 1909, he used chemicals called phenol and formaldehyde to create the world's first truly synthetic (human-made) plastic. It was called Bakelite. Unlike the other plastics, Bakelite did not come from any substance found in nature. It was an entirely new chemical creation.

Bakelite was so much stronger and longer-lasting than other plastics. It was also much cheaper to make and sell. Factories all over the world began producing this new plastic. It was used for everything from clocks, radios, telephones, and jewellery, to children's toys, electric guitars, and the first machine guns used in World War I.

▼ Telephones made from Bakelite were once very popular for ordinary, everyday use. Today they are valuable collectors' items or antiques.

# So many kinds of plastic, so many uses

▲ Many medical supplies are made of disposable plastics.

In the 1920s and 1930s, many new kinds of plastic were developed and put to use. Over time, scientists working for chemical companies worked out new ways to use and improve these plastics.

Formica (a hard, strong plastic with a shiny surface) became a popular material for kitchen worktops. PVC (polyvinyl chloride) was used to make pipes for plumbing, gutters, shower curtains, and flooring. Melamine cups, bowls, and plates didn't break if you dropped them. Saran cling film covered foods and kept them from spoiling. Vinyl could be used to make anything from window frames and medical supplies, to articles of clothing.

Polyester was another plastic that could be used to make wrinkle-free, stain-resistant clothing. Scientists found that acrylic could imitate fabrics such as wool. It could also be used to create certain kinds of paint and a type of clear, shatter-resistant "glass".

## The invention of nylon

Wallace Hume Carothers (1896–1937) worked for the DuPont Chemical Corporation in the United States. While he was trying to find substitutes for rubber, he invented nylon and neoprene. Nylon is a plastic that can be drawn out into long, thin fibres, like silk. It is lightweight, strong, and long-lasting. Manufacturers use nylon to make toothbrush bristles, rope, tents, parachutes, luggage, and tights.

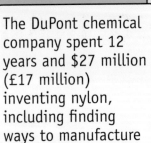

**A big investment**

The DuPont chemical company spent 12 years and $27 million (£17 million) inventing nylon, including finding ways to manufacture it and use it.

◀ Laptop covers, wetsuits for swimmers and divers, and Halloween masks are all made of neoprene. This soft, rubbery plastic is also used for wrist, elbow, knee, and ankle supports.

 Space exploration has been made possible in part by the invention of plastics.

**One giant leap** ✓

When US astronaut Neil Armstrong walked on the Moon in 1969, he was wearing a space suit that was part Teflon.

## New discoveries and new inventions

Sometimes it took years for teams of scientists to work out how to use a plastic that had been invented or discovered much earlier. For instance, Roy Plunkett was working at the DuPont Chemical Corporation in 1938. He created a slippery plastic coating called Teflon. It wasn't until the 1960s that manufacturers found a way to use Teflon to coat kitchen pots and pans, so that food wouldn't stick to them!

In the 1960s and 1970s, scientists explored many new chemical combinations and processes for creating and working with plastics. In the 1980s, a plastic called Kevlar (invented by American Stephanie Kwolek) was used to make bullet-proof body armour for police officers and members of the military.

Scientists also worked to develop plastics that could withstand extremely high temperatures. These new plastics were used to make parts for cars, aeroplanes, and spacecraft.

Other new plastics worked better for computers, mobile phones, and MP3 players. Some are used to make glasses and contact lenses. Some provide layers of insulation or protection for electrical wires, machines, and equipment.

Scientists all over the world are still experimenting. They are always improving or replacing old plastics with new and better plastics.

◀ In the 1800s, US inventors John Jacob Bausch and Henry Lomb discovered that spectacle frames could be made from inexpensive plastics, rather than costly metals. Today spectacle lenses and contact lenses are also made of plastic.

# Why plastics are special

▲ **Plastics come in many colours, shapes, and sizes.**

Over the last century, plastic products have gradually replaced hundreds of products that used to be made with other materials such as paper, wood, stone, metal, glass, pottery, and leather. This is because plastics have some special qualities. They can be moulded into any shape or size. They can be dyed any colour – or left clear.

Plastics can be made softer, harder, or stretchier than other natural materials. They don't break as easily as glass, pottery, or bones. They don't rot or decay, so they last longer than paper or wood products. They don't rust like metal, or get mouldy like leather.

Most plastics are cheap and easy to make. They are disposable. We don't have to repair plastic items that are broken. We don't need to clean plastic items that have been exposed to germs and diseases. Plastic items can be easily replaced.

Unlike water and metal, plastic does not conduct electricity. In other words, electricity cannot travel through it. So plastic works as an **insulator**, to protect people and things from damage caused by lightning or power surges.

Most importantly, plastic does not dissolve or break down in water. It doesn't react to the chemicals in soap, alcohol, petrol, and other substances. So plastic can be used to make containers to carry these things!

## Warning!

Plastics are not always cheap. It depends on what they are made from. Plastics made from **petroleum** (oil) are becoming increasingly expensive. This is because there is only a limited supply of petroleum chemicals and they are **non-renewable**. It is important to **recycle** and reuse these plastics.

▼ These wires are covered with a protective layer of plastic.

# What plastics are made of

▲ **This scientist is checking the quality of sheets of a plastic polymer called Makrolon. Light shines better through Makrolon than through glass.**

Most of the chemical ingredients used to make plastic come from petroleum, although some come from plant and wood fibres. Scientists take these chemicals from nature or recreate them in a **laboratory** in order to form plastics.

16

All plastics are made up of groups of **hydrocarbon molecules**. These are molecules that have thousands and thousands of hydrogen **atoms** and carbon atoms. Some also have oxygen, nitrogen, chlorine, or sulphur atoms.

## How plastics work

Small hydrocarbon molecules called monomers are joined together with other monomers to create large molecules called polymers. Scientists arrange these polymers in long repeating chains, ladders, rings, or branches. What makes one plastic different from another is the number of polymers it has, the type of polymers, the combination of different polymers, and the way these polymers are linked together.

▼ Plastics are made of hydrocarbons – molecules formed by hydrogen and carbon atoms joined together in groups or chains like these.

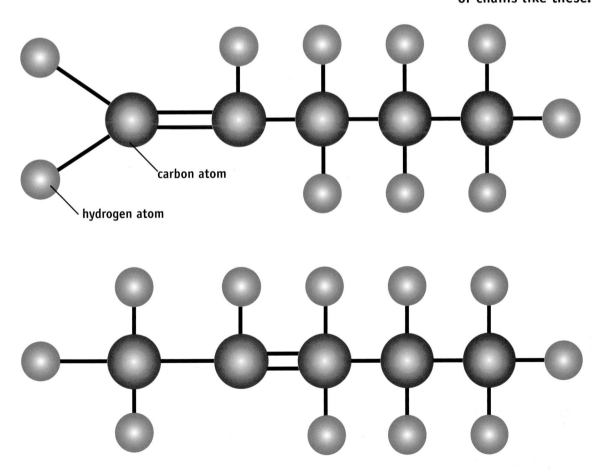

carbon atom

hydrogen atom

17

▲ Polyurethane is
an example of a
thermoset plastic.
It is used to make
things like car parts
and skateboard
wheels.

## Grouping plastics

The many different kinds of plastic can be organized
into groups or categories. These categories might
describe the main ingredients of the plastic or the
quality of the plastic. They can also describe the
characteristics of the plastic and what kind of products
it is used for. Most of the time, however, scientists put
plastics into one of two categories: thermoset plastics
and thermoplastics.

## Thermoset plastics

All plastics are created by combining the chemical
ingredients and heating them until they turn into a
liquid. This liquid plastic is poured into moulds. When
the liquid cools down, it hardens and takes the shape of
the moulds.

Thermoset plastics can only be heated once, during the process in which they are created. Once they have cooled, they stay in the shape in which they have been made. If a thermoset plastic is exposed to heat again, it melts into a gooey chemical mess that cannot be reused.

## Thermoplastics

Thermoplastics can be heated and reheated, shaped and reshaped. A thermoplastic cup, for instance, can be melted down and remade into a bowl.

▼ This hula-hoop is made of polyethylene. Polyethylene is a thermoplastic. It is the most widely used plastic in the world.

# How plastics are made

▲ Plastic is made in large quantities in factories like this one.

Plastics are made in factories all over the world. Manufacturers (companies that make things to sell) follow special recipes or formulas to create the specific kind of plastic they want. They mix all the chemical ingredients together in giant tanks. A machine like a blender adds both heat and pressure as the mixture spins around inside. At this stage, the monomers are joining to each other to become polymers.

Manufacturers add other chemicals that will give the plastic its colour or make it fire-resistant or extra-shiny – whatever important qualities they want the plastic to have.

The plastic that comes through this process looks like little beads or pellets. These pellets will be heated until they melt into a liquid. The liquid goes into a mould that gives the plastic its shape.

Different kinds of moulds produce different kinds of shapes – from bracelets to toys to computer keyboards to cups, bowls, and plates. As the plastic cools, it hardens. Sometimes a special protective coating is added to the finished product.

▼ **These plastic pellets will be melted down into liquid plastic and poured into moulds of different shapes and sizes.**

# Recycling plastic

▲ Plastic drinking bottles can always be reused and recycled.

Today we produce and use 20 times more plastic than we did 50 years ago. About a billion tonnes of that plastic has just been thrown away. Other types of rubbish – such as food waste, garden waste, or items made of natural substances such as cotton, wool, or wood – will eventually rot. These things break down into pieces, eaten by tiny bacteria. However, most bacteria do not eat plastic! Plastic does not easily break down. It will last for hundreds and maybe thousands of years.

# How recycling works

Since the 1990s, people all over the world have been learning to reuse and recycle plastic. Plastic bags, bottles, and other items are collected and sent to recycling plants. There, workers separate the plastics by type and category. The plastics are shredded, washed, and dried. Then machines melt the plastics back into a liquid form. They filter out any bits and pieces of rubbish. Once the plastic has cooled and hardened, it is shredded into pellets and sold back to plastic manufacturing companies.

## Biodegradable

If something can be dissolved or broken down by bacteria, it is called biodegradable. Most plastics are not biodegradable. They do not break down naturally over time. They have to be recycled.

## Bottles and more bottles

People in the United Kingdom buy billions of plastic water bottles each year. Only three out of every ten of these bottles makes its way to a recycling plant. The rest are piled up in landfills and rubbish dumps.

▼ Many plastics can be sent to recycling plants like this one.

23

► Recycling plastic can
be more difficult and
more expensive than
making new plastic.

## Problems with recycling

The process of recycling can be expensive. It takes a lot
of time and energy to sort the different kinds of plastic.
They can't all be combined, even if they are the same
kind of plastic, because some are different colours or
have different chemical ingredients that don't mix well.
There are a lot of plastics that simply can't be recycled.
It is too difficult and complicated to break them down
– or when they have been broken down, they can't be
reused.

## Things you can do

1. Refill and reuse your plastic water bottles, instead of buying new ones. When it's time to discard the bottles, make sure they go into a recycling bin.
2. Reuse plastic shopping bags or take re-usable cloth bags to the shops.
3. Donate used plastic toys to charity shops, instead of throwing them away.
4. Take plastic containers to schools or craft centres, where they can be reused in creative ways.
5. Buy products that are made from recycled materials or that have very little packaging. If possible, the packaging should be made from ingredients that can be recycled.

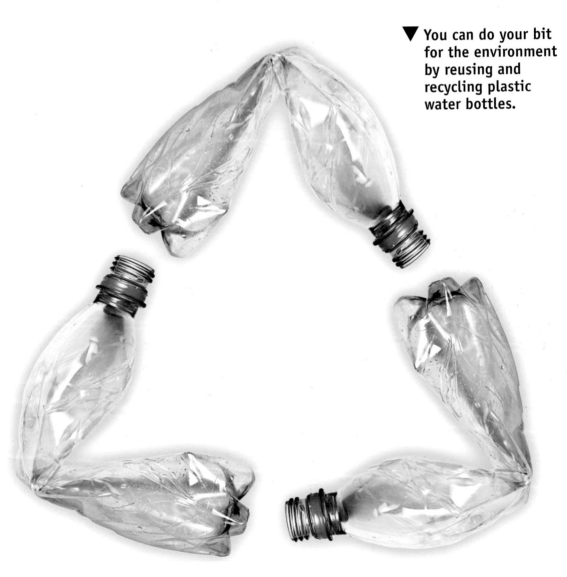

▼ You can do your bit for the environment by reusing and recycling plastic water bottles.

# The future of plastic

▲ Plastic litter like this can build up in lakes and rivers, posing a major threat to fish, birds, and other wildlife.

Many people are becoming concerned about the amount of plastic – and the kinds of plastic – that are a part of our daily lives. This is not just because of the amount of plastic that we throw away. Some plastics have been found to contain chemicals that cause **cancer** and other diseases. These chemicals are released when the plastic is microwaved, heated, or burned at a rubbish dump.

# Making it work

The plastic rings that hold six-packs of soft drinks together have caused a lot of damage to the environment – especially to the fish, birds, and other animals that get caught in the plastic loops that people have thrown away. Scientists have created a new formula or recipe for this plastic, so that it is now photodegradable. This means that in sunlight, the plastic rings dissolve into powder after a few months.

Today scientists are working hard to find new ways to recycle and break down the kind of plastics that are filling up our landfill sites. They are also trying to create new plastics that are safer and healthier for us and better for the environment.

**Searching for solutions**

Scientists are now experimenting with ways to make plastics from safer, more natural ingredients such as fructose – a form of sugar!

▼ **This packaging is made of a biodegradable plastic wrapper. If it is placed in a landfill, rubbish pile, or compost heap, it will eventually break down and dissolve completely.**

# Timeline

(These dates are often approximations.)

**1800s–2000**
Scientists develop fire-resistant plastics made of liquid crystal polymers.

1800

**1862**
Alexander Parkes introduces Parkesine, the first human-made plastic.

**1856**
Alfred Critchlow and Samuel Peck invent shellac.

1860

1850

**1869**
John Wesley Hyatt creates celluloid, the first US plastic.

**1872**
Eugen Baumann invents polyvinyl chloride or PVC.

1870

1880

**1930–1931**
Wallace Hume Carothers and his team develop neoprene as a replacement for rubber.

**1926**
Walter Semon invents a version of PVC called vinyl.

1930

**1933**
Ralph Wiley creates polyvinylidene chloride or Saran (cling film).

**1936**
Acrylic is invented.

**1937**
Otto Bayer and his co-workers patent plastics called polyurethanes.

**1960s–1970s**
Scientists invent a variety of thermoplastic substances that can be used in place of fabrics and metals.

1970

1960

**1980s**
Japanese scientists perfect plastics that withstand extremely high temperatures and can be used for cars, aeroplanes, and spacecraft.

**1980s**
A plastic called Kevlar is used to make body armour for the US military.

1980

1990

This symbol shows where there is a change of scale in the timeline, or where a long period of time with no noted events has been left out.

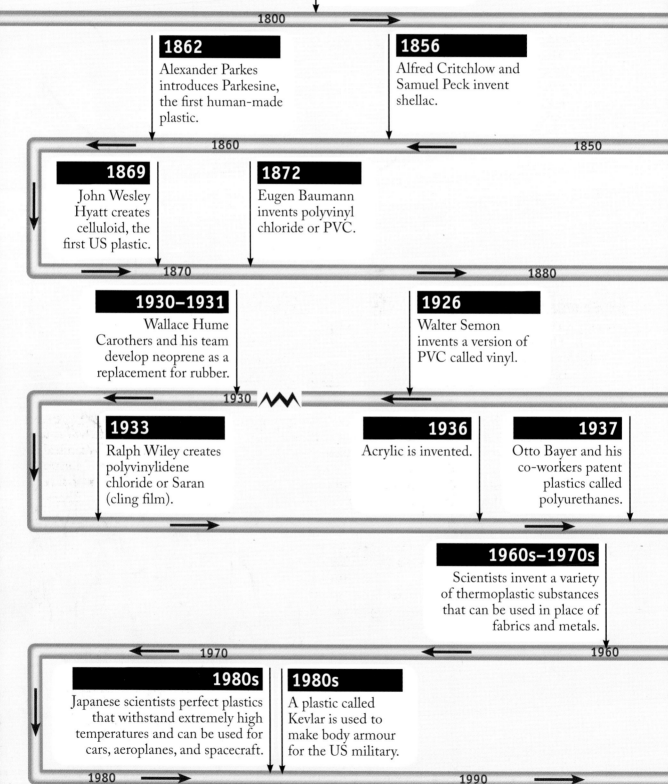

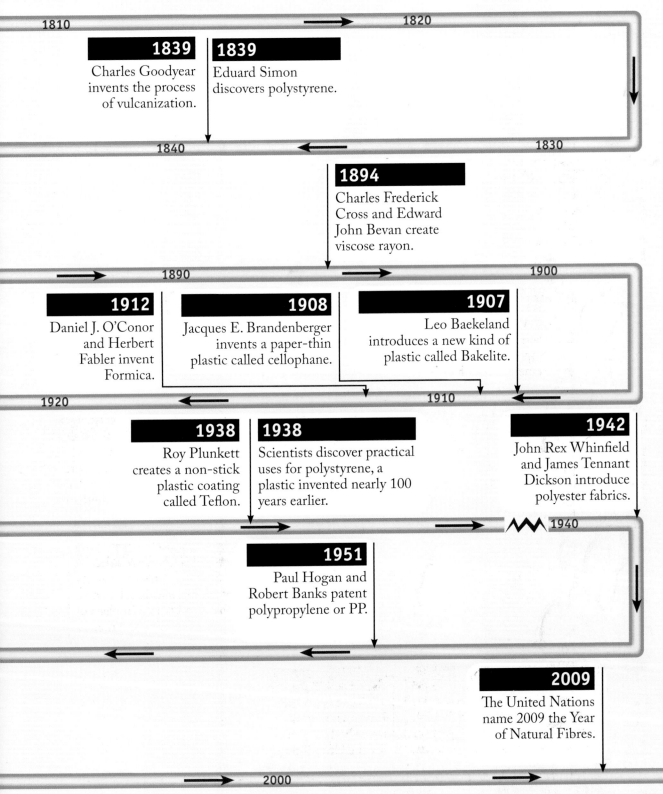

1810    →    1820

**1839**
Charles Goodyear invents the process of vulcanization.

**1839**
Eduard Simon discovers polystyrene.

1840    ←    1830

**1894**
Charles Frederick Cross and Edward John Bevan create viscose rayon.

1890    →    1900

**1912**
Daniel J. O'Conor and Herbert Fabler invent Formica.

**1908**
Jacques E. Brandenberger invents a paper-thin plastic called cellophane.

**1907**
Leo Baekeland introduces a new kind of plastic called Bakelite.

1920    ←    1910

**1938**
Roy Plunkett creates a non-stick plastic coating called Teflon.

**1938**
Scientists discover practical uses for polystyrene, a plastic invented nearly 100 years earlier.

**1942**
John Rex Whinfield and James Tennant Dickson introduce polyester fabrics.

1940

**1951**
Paul Hogan and Robert Banks patent polypropylene or PP.

**2009**
The United Nations name 2009 the Year of Natural Fibres.

2000    →

29

# Glossary

**atom** tiniest part of an element, a substance that cannot be made any smaller

**cancer** disease in which some cells grow very quickly, forming lumps which may spread through the body

**characteristic** feature that makes a substance special or different from others

**chemical** substance that can be made into other substances by changing its atoms or molecules

**chemistry** study of substances, what they are made of, and how they react to each other

**disposable** made to be thrown away after use

**hydrocarbon** molecule made of hydrogen and carbon atoms

**insulator** something that surrounds and protects an object from heat and electricity

**laboratory** place used for science experiments and tests

**molecule** tiny particle composed of one or more atoms

**non-renewable** something that cannot be replaced once it runs out

**patent** rights to an invention for a limited period of time. The patent allows the owner to make money from an invention without competition from other companies.

**petroleum** an oil found under ground or under the seabed

**polystyrene** a plastic first found in the Turkish sweet gum tree, now produced in a chemical form

**recycle** use over again, sometimes in a new way

**resistant** keeps something (such as water) out

**synthetic** substance that is human-made (from chemicals), not found in nature

**vulcanization** treating rubber with sulphur to make it strong, elastic, and waterproof

# Find out more

## Books

*A Plastic Toy* (How It's Made), Susan Barraclough (Franklin Watts, 2006)
*Recycling* (Go Facts: Environment), (A & C Black, 2007)
*Plastics* (Re-using and Recycling), Ruth Thomson (Franklin Watts, 2006)
*What Happens When We Recycle Plastic?*, Jillian Powell (Franklin Watts, 2008)

## Website

**www.recycle-more.co.uk**
Click on the "Schools" tab on this website for some recycling tips and activities.

## Place to visit

Bakelite Museum
Orchard Mill
Williton
Somerset TA4 4NS
**www.bakelitemuseum.co.uk**
This museum has the largest collection of plastic objects in the UK.

# Index